SUCCESSFUL

MARKETING

CW01068349

Mike Levy

60 Minutes Success Skills Series

First published 1998 by
David Grant Publishing Limited
80 Ridgeway, Pembury, Kent TN2 4EZ United Kingdom

60 Minutes Success Skills Series is an imprint of
David Grant Publishing Limited

British Library Cataloguing in Publication Data
A CIP record for this book is available from the British Library

ISBN 1-901306-10-0

Cover design: Steve Haynes
Text design: Graham Rich
Production Editor: Paul Stringer
Typeset in Futura by
Archetype IT Ltd, web site http://www.archetype-it.com

Printed and bound in Great Britain by
T.J. International, Padstow, Cornwall

This book is printed on acid-free paper

*The publishers accept no responsibility for any investment or financial decisions
made on the basis of the information in this book. Readers are advised always to
consult a qualified financial adviser.*

*All names mentioned in the text have been changed to protect the identity of the
business people involved. Any resemblance to existing companies or people is
entirely coincidental.*

CONTENTS

ABOUT *SUCCESSFUL MARKETING*

Can you learn how to get to grips with marketing in one hour? The answer is a resounding "YES". This book sets out all of the key issues and will give you a blueprint which you can apply to marketing just about anything!

The 60 Minutes Success Skills Series is written for people with neither the time nor the patience to trawl through acres of jargon, management-speak and page-filling waffle. Like all the books in the series, *Successful Marketing* has been written in the belief that you can learn all you really need to know quickly and without hassle. The aim is to distil the essential, practical advice you can use straight away.

How to use this book

The message here is "It's OK to skim". Feel free to flick through to find the help you most need. This book is a collection of hands-on tips which will help you to spot any shortcomings you might have and show you how to turn them into strengths. You **can** become the slick marketeer you've always wanted to be.

Successful Marketing has been written to dip into. You don't have to read it all at one go or follow every tip to the letter. If you're really pushed for time, you could skip through the book following the boxed features. These summarise each of the points covered by prompting you to think about an issue, and then giving you action points which are backed up with lists of handy tips to keep you on the right track.

GOOD LUCK!

The author

Mike Levy is a freelance business journalist, author, trainer and grants consultant. His training courses include interviewing skills, marketing, customer care, stress management and EU funding.

For more details contact: mike@levy-writer.demon.co.uk

Acknowledgement

Many thanks are due to Mike Ramsay, director of Direct Marketing Concepts Ltd for all his help in the preparation of this book.

What's in this chapter for you

Blowing away the marketing myths
What does marketing involve?
Taking control
Marketing marketing

Blowing away the marketing myths

There can be few areas of business that are so maligned as marketing. In some ways it's the fault of the "image" of professional marketing people, with their flashy designer clothes, swish offices and self-serving "marketing speak". Forget them. What you need to realise is that marketing is essential for survival and growth – and it's a tool which is easily within your grasp.

> **❝** *Assuming that the product is OK, 99 per cent of business success is down to marketing. You can have the greatest idea, product or service – but no customers, no future.* **❞**
> **– Simon Wells, self-made millionaire in furniture retailing**

Simon appreciates the value and importance of the marketing function. Marketing is the key to **profit** and **survival**!

Do you have negative feelings about marketing? If you do, it's a fair bet you can't think of any successful companies which aren't fully committed to marketing their products and services. So, why is that?

Marketing is an essential function of any business – and the better you are at it, the more your business will prosper. Here are a few basic truths about marketing.

1. Marketing is for all businesses – big and small

Marketing is about customers – the life blood of every organisation, from schools to steel mills, from window cleaners to merchant banks.

2. A business cannot survive the competitive pressures of the new century without a proper marketing strategy

Times are getting tougher and markets are getting wider. You need to get your message across.

> 66 *Marketing these days is like trying to make a speech in the middle of the World Cup Finals* 99
> **– Dee Coles, college principal**

3. Marketing is about much more than just advertising

Advertising is one of the weapons in the marketeer's armoury – but it is by no means the only one, nor is it always the most effective one.

4. You can afford to develop your marketing strategy

This point might best have been called "you cannot afford *not* to develop your marketing strategy!"

> 66 *All my marketing is free. I work on word-of-mouth reputation, having an eye-catching sign outside my office and giving a lot of talks on local radio.* 99
> **– Barry Foster, energy management consultant**

5. Marketing can be simple

You don't need to be an expert or spend lots of valuable cash on consultants. Once you have read this book you will already be on the road to improving your business profile in the market.

> 66 *The marketing people would have us believe it's all an exact science. In fact, marketing is basically just about being more customer-aware – listen to them, that's all you need to do.* 99
> **– Julia Fender, haberdasher**

6. Marketing is not just someone else's responsibility – it's yours too

Business success and marketing go hand in hand. Since marketing is fundamentally about keeping the customers happy, it follows that everybody in the organisation has a role to play – surly receptionists, sloppy promotional material and poor production quality will certainly not win you any new customers or help you to keep the ones you've got. Marketing is something you must involve yourself in, whatever your function in a company.

> Do you agree with the last point? Is it always true in your situation?

❤ *We ran a three-person partnership and I always thought that marketing was Sally's responsibility. We left it to her to promote the business, deal with the advertising, and come up with new ways of getting more customers. When Sally left us, Bob and I really panicked. What did we know about marketing? But when we looked at it, we had been marketing for years – going to client's parties, talking to introducers, selling new services to existing clients . . .* ❝
– Graham David, Chartered Accountant

> From what you have read, think through your current attitude to marketing. What do you now do that could be classed as "marketing"? How can you improve what you already do well?

What does marketing involve?

Marketing involves anything that helps towards making your customers more satisfied. Remember:

No satisfied customers = No business
. . . there's no truer maxim

Customer satisfaction is only achieved when they get what they want, in the right place, and at a price they are willing to pay. Anyone in your business who helps this process is involved in marketing.

Notice, then, that marketing is all to do with: the Product or service you sell; the Place where it is sold and distributed; the Price of the product or service; and how you Promote the product. These are often referred to as the 4Ps of marketing. We will find out more about the 4Ps later.

Do you have any input in the product you sell, its price, where you sell it, how you tell the world about it? If the answer is "Yes" to any of these points, you are already involved in marketing.

If you are in business the chances are you are already a pretty good marketing person – although maybe you didn't know it!

Just remember: *Marketing is the creative process of satisfying customer needs, profitably and effectively.*

Taking control

You should now be convinced that marketing is indeed part of your responsibility. You will also know how much customer care and satisfaction have become the keystone to successful business in this decade. Customer-led businesses are the ones most likely to succeed and that's where marketing comes in.

Think about these questions in relation to your organisation.

- ❏ *Could we be more customer-oriented than we are?*
- ❏ *Do we always know what our customers think about our product or services?*
- ❏ *Are we always ready to face competition from new or existing businesses?*
- ❏ *Are we producing a product or providing a service that people want now and will still want in the future?*
- ❏ *Is our product or service getting to the customers we need – or are we badly located or spending too much money on getting the goods to market?*
- ❏ *Do we make the most of our successes? Does the market know about us and what we do?*
- ❏ *Are we charging the right prices for our customers and our own bottom line?*
- ❏ *Have we got the right balance between our price and the quality of the product or service we sell?*
- ❏ *Have our staff been properly trained to ensure that customers get the best we can offer?*
- ❏ *Do we do all that we can to persuade people to buy our products?*

Each of these questions is a marketing question. If any of them trouble you, you should take action – now!

Marketing marketing

> ❝ *I turned my company around by creating a "marketing first" organisation. However, I could only do this once I'd persuaded my colleagues how important it really is.* ❞
> **– Hamid Sarawi, CEO of security products company**

If you need to "sell" the benefits of marketing to others (or even yourself), here are some great selling points. Marketing helps:

- ○ *you to overcome shrinking traditional markets*
- ○ *your company or organisation to survive and prosper*
- ○ *generate new business*
- ○ *consolidate existing business*
- ○ *keep you one step ahead of your customers and competition.*

Easy ways to "put on a marketing hat"

1. Start thinking of marketing as "potential profit" – it's the ultimate motivator.
2. Look for ways to take greater control of marketing in your organisation.
3. Start talking to other marketing people – how do they think?
4. Start looking at your existing marketing (if any) much more critically – what are the biggest weaknesses and the greatest strengths?
5. Take a fresh look at your customers – who are they, where are they, and why do they buy from you?
6. Start thinking about your product – what is it, and what does (or should) make it more popular with customers?
7. Look at your competition – what are they doing (a) better and (b) worse than you in marketing their products?
8. Get rid of any prejudices you still have about marketing – you can't afford them! Start persuading your colleagues that marketing is everyone's business.

What's in this chapter for you

> *Know thy customers*
> *Customer focus*
> *Identify your customers*
> *Market segmentation*

> " *One of the cardinal rules in marketing is to know your customers better than the back of your hand. Never second guess them. Don't claim to speak for them. Just get off your butt and find out.* "
> **– Jane Sellars, founder of a successful mail order company**

Know thy customers

The first stage in marketing (after you have persuaded yourself that it is important) is to do some research. The most important thing you need to know is who your customers are.

> What do you know about your customers? Do you think you know enough? How could you find out more?

Think about your current customers and who your potential new customers might be. Ask yourself:

○ *Who are they?*
○ *Where are they?*
○ *How many of them are there?*
○ *What do they want now and in future?*
○ *What do they currently need and how will those needs change?*

> " *When we did a survey we discovered that our customers were not who we'd thought. It all came as quite a surprise but it helped us target our marketing much more effectively. We gave up advertising in the tabloids, for instance, and developed a nice, stylish promotion in the local up-market magazine. Business has been booming ever since.* "
> **– Mike Silver, coach operator.**

The more you know about customers, the easier it is to market effectively to them. You can't know enough about them, so don't be complacent when analysing your customers.

Customer focus

If you believe the "right" product will sell itself, read what Ben Reynolds has to say.

> ❝ We spent a lot of time, money and energy on making our products the best in town. The trouble soon began. OK, we had a few loyal customers but not enough to pay the bills. Within a couple of months we had eaten into our overdraft and the finance people started ringing alarm bells. Within six months, the banks called in their debts and we were bust. "If only the public knew what they were missing," we said to ourselves. ❞
> **Ben Reynolds, MD of a print firm**

If only the public knew what they were missing – this is a sure sign of an organisation focused on its products rather than its customers, an untenable situation. A customer-focused organisation:

- ○ *only develops the products its customers demand*
- ○ *spends a lot of resources on marketing and customer liaison*
- ○ *believes in the "ask first, then supply" way of doing business.*

A customer-focused organisation is marketing led. This how the majority of today's successful companies are run. So many commercial failures are due to product focus. Think of the Sinclair C5 electric car, the Betamax video system or the numerous short-lived newspapers which have been launched.

Is your organisation product or customer focused? Your job is to turn your business into a customer-focused organisation. Think about how you can get you and your colleagues to talk more about customers and perhaps less about the product.
Remember: put the customer first!

Identify your customers

So, who are these important customers of yours? What kind of customer records, if any, are kept by your organisation which could help you answer this question? Do you have existing customers listed on a database? Among other things, what you need to know is where they live, and what type of people they are. Customers come in all shapes and sizes so don't overlook any sector as you put together a picture of who they are.

Your contact with customers can vary. For any market to exist, however, there must be some kind of contact. This can be face to face, or by mail, telephone or fax. Another growing sector of customers is accessed through the internet.

How do you make contact with customers? Can it be improved? Can you do so in new ways?

❝ *I run a shop and used to think that I only met customers over the counter. This is true of existing customers but new customers are everywhere. I sell carpets and have learnt always to be customer aware. Wherever I am, there are potential customers – at my kids' school, in the pub, at parties, on the bus. I never go anywhere without my business card and I've always got something to show a potential buyer.* ❞

– Reg Robinson, carpet dealer

In Reg's case, any contact he makes is a potential customer. This doesn't mean that you have to become a round-the-clock, pain-in-the-pants sales person who clears the pub in 30 seconds flat, but it does mean you should be aware that, when it comes to customers, "the truth IS out there". The trick is to recognise a potential customer when you see one.

Market segmentation

This sounds like marketing-speak and so it is. The concept is very simple: your customers are not likely to be an homogenous whole but split into different social classes, ages, occupation types and locations.

Market segmentation tells you a lot about how to reach your customers by identifying who they are and what they are likely to want. For instance, if you sell lace underwear you wouldn't promote your wares through a series of adverts in *The Polar Explorer* – unless you know something very special about some of your customers! You will also be aware that people who live in different regions tend to like different things.

Identifying your market segments is part of a constant information gathering process your company should be fully committed to. We will see later how to encourage customers to tell you about themselves.

> **Market segmentation sounds very complicated but, if you have the right information, it will only take you a few minutes to assess how your customers differ. Think about how your customers could be classified into identifiable sectors.**

When thinking about your customers ask:

- *Who are the key decision-makers?*
- *What characteristics do your main customers possess? For instance, the basic information could include:*
    age, sex and marital status
    social class or group
    children
    typical occupations and income levels
    interests
    geographical location.

Now think about (or find out) how many of your existing customers fit into each of the categories you have identified. You should do the same exercise for potential new customers.

Armed with this detail about your customers, you can target your marketing much more effectively.

❝ *We were very worried about falling school rolls. Pupils from our traditional feeder schools were either going elsewhere or there were fewer of them. We decided to carry out a thorough market analysis – where were our potential pupils? Where were they going if not to us? What were they looking for? What family backgrounds did they*

tend to have? After we had done this, we discovered that we were losing out on attracting a lot of children from higher income homes who lived in certain areas of the city. We targeted our publicity and promotional visits on those areas – their shops, libraries, local feeder schools and even nurseries.
Now our roll is rising once more. **99**
– Head teacher of a secondary school

Remember: You cannot know too much about your customers. Take market segmentation seriously.

Sure-fire ways to understand your customers:

1. Take stock of your existing customers – who are they, what do they want now and what will they expect in the future? Divide your customers into market segments.
2. Make sure your organisation is customer focused and not product focused. Start thinking that every contact is a potential customer.
3. Start keeping more detailed customer records. Keep separate records for every type of customer contact: face-to-face, mail order, telephone sales and so on.
4. Think of ways to make customers tell you more about themselves – e.g. design questionnaires and encourage responses with "loyalty schemes" or prize draws.
5. Do some research on new, potential customers – what market segments do they fall into?
6. Never, ever, be satisfied with the information you have about your customers – keep trying to improve it and get more.

What's in this chapter for you

> **Where you get your information**
> **Internal and external audits (PEST)**
> **Primary research**
> **Analysing your findings**

> ❝ *Market research means a lot of standing around on street corners with clipboards. It's a lot of effort for minimal gain* ❞
> **– Geoff Sidebotham, warehouse manager**

Market research

> What do you think market research is all about? Have you done it? Do you plan to do it? Would you rather leave it to others?

For many people, the very term "market research" fills them with foreboding: the thought of the time and effort needed can be overwhelming.

> ❝ *Market research is something we know would be valuable because our sales are diving at the moment, but we just cannot afford it.* ❞
> **– Daniel Darling, electrical supplier**

Daniel's comment is typical. Hiring a market research consultancy can be very costly, but you can do so much yourself without expending a huge amount of time and money.

Market research simply means the gathering together of market data which is then recorded and analysed. Why do it? Market research helps in two key ways:

○ *First, it helps you target your products and services much more accurately and profitably.*
○ *Second, it helps you monitor and control the marketing process much more carefully, thereby cutting out wasted effort and saving money.*

You don't have to be a big organisation to use market research. Anyone can do it. It involves the following key stages:

(1) Ask: What do I need to know?

> **❝** *Our market research exercise started with a team brainstorm. We began by asking where do we, as a company, want to be in five years' time.* **❞**
> **– David West, MD of a small freight carrier**

(2) Clarify your marketing *aims* and *objectives*. "What's the difference?" you might be tempted to ask. Well:

○ *Aims = where are we heading?*
○ *Objectives = how are we going to achieve the aims?*

> **❝** *Our aim was easy – to be the biggest freight carrier in our region within three years. Currently we were number eight. Our objectives had to be quantified of course – to expand our regional customer base by 24 per cent within two years and to take up to 4 per cent of the national market.* **❞**
> **– David West**

Clarify your aims in marketing. Then, work out your measurable objectives. These can be measured in pounds, sales, market share, numbers of customers, rates of growth – whatever is appropriate – but objectives must be measurable.

---

(3) Set out clear terms of reference for the research needed. Ask: "What data needs to be collected?" Market research can be time consuming so make sure you know *exactly* what you need to know. Time spent in thinking this through can save a lot of hassle later on.

> **❝** *Our terms of reference were fairly clear: we needed to explore the regional marketplace within its four main segments. We needed to know the size of total business, recent rates of growth, market share of our main competitors, customer awareness of ourselves and the competition.* **❞**
> **– David West**

(4) Start collecting the data. The golden rule here is: *Do it systematically.* We'll come back to this below.

(5) Analyse and interpret what you have found. This is obviously the key stage. If you cannot derive any ideas from the research you've done, then the effort will have been wasted.

> **Start to think about these key stages of market research.**
> **Discuss them with colleagues. Work out when and how you are**
> **going to implement them.**

Let's look more closely at stage 4, collecting data. There are two main sources: these are "primary data" and "secondary data". Secondary data already exists – it's out there just waiting for you. It is published in directories, journals, books, articles, fact sheets, statistics and so on.

Finding sources of secondary information doesn't take long – once you have put your mind to it. A very good place to start is your local library, especially if it has a commercial section.

Where you get your information

This obviously depends very much on the nature of the business you are in – your local paper is unlikely to offer much help if you're trying to shift that 200 kilos of weapons grade plutonium you've had in your shed for ages – but some ready sources of information include:

- ○ *telephone directories and business directories*
- ○ *local and national newspapers*
- ○ *specialist journals*
- ○ *government information services*
- ○ *chambers of commerce*
- ○ *commercial data banks*
- ○ *research institutions and industry lead bodies*
- ○ *the year book of a particular profession or trade association.*

In addition, there's the internet. This is an amazing source of information. It takes time to sift through all the garbage but, with patience, you are more than likely to come up with exactly the information you need.

And don't forget to study the competition, especially if they are doing well – find out what makes them successful.

> ❝ We wanted to test the market for clients in the complementary medicine field. How to begin? I had a brainwave. Check out all the journals read by practitioners and patients in this field. A little research unveiled around 15 magazines and journals. They tell you about latest trends; what your competitors might be doing. It's also a great way to get to potential clients in that segment. ❞
>
> **Anil Desai, medical supplier**

Take a few moments to think. Where can you get the data and background information to support your marketing strategy?

Internal audit

Don't forget to look closely at your existing business arena. The best market trends are often being shaped under your nose. Take time to do an internal audit of your company's business. If you keep sales records (and you should) on computer, you can get software programs which print out sales trends. It is important to see what segments of your market are growing and those which need stimulating.

An internal audit should include:

○ *your market share and that of your competitors*
○ *internal sales figures divided by market segments (for instance, the growth in sales for customers over 35, or living in the north, or with children and so on)*
○ *an evaluation of your price, your product, where you are selling your product and how you are promoting it (see the later chapters covering the 4Ps)*
○ *the number of new enquiries, complaints, comments and so on.*

Make a list of the marketing information you would include in your internal audit.

External audit (PEST)

You should also carry out an external audit. This looks at the influences on your product or service of factors outside your immediate control. The classic way to remember these external influences is PEST: P (politics), E (economics), S (Social), T (technology).

No business is an island The best of business plans can come unstuck when things in the outside world change. Think of the impact on your organisation of, say, a change of government, a collapse of the pound, a new law banning your activities, some new invention that makes your product obsolete. Marketing is about the future. To be ready for change, you need to be aware of the influences on your business from the external environment. Let's look at PEST more closely.

Politics

Our politicians and law makers have immense power over the way we do business. They can and do have a direct effect on:

○ *interest rates*
○ *regulations governing the manufacture or use of your product*
○ *taxation, grants and subsidies*
○ *export and import regulations and trading relations with other countries*
○ *laws on how you describe your product, laws on advertising, and so on.*

Economics

We all operate in an economic environment. Your sales will depend directly on:

○ *the level of employment*
○ *the overall growth rate of the economy*
○ *taxes and other deductions affecting disposable income*
○ *recession or recovery*
○ *the cost of borrowing money.*

A very important factor here is the economic cycle. For instance, the years 1985–8 and 1994–7 were definitely periods of growth and recovery in the USA and Europe. But there were lean years, such as the recessions of 1979–82 and 1989–93. In a recession, business takes a dive, customers rein in their spending, jobs are lost and companies go bust. Past recessions have been caused by oil price hikes, wars, business crashes in overseas markets, stock exchange collapse, etc.

You should spend at least some time every week reading the business sections in the newspapers. Find out what the pundits think about the coming cycle of recession or recovery. (Unfortunately, there are lots of these "experts" and they are not always right, so don't shut up shop as soon as you fear the worst. The idea is to be aware of what's going on – it could save your business or even open up new opportunities for you.)

Social

Buying habits change with fashion, tastes and differing social attitudes. Changes in society have had significant effects on a whole range of goods and services: these can range from "green" issues to women's liberation, from changes in family values to our attitudes to religion and work. Many companies have made it big by spotting changes in society before they happen on a large scale. Social change can easily do your business harm, or good. Your job is to be aware. Read the papers and talk to customers. Keep your finger on the market pulse.

Technological

There has never been a time when technological change has moved faster. This is especially true in communications, computers and leisure products. The implications are well beyond the scope of this book and you are probably already painfully aware of them. Again, you need to keep abreast of developments as far as humanly possible.

> **"** We thought we had a world-beating can opener until someone revolutionised the design and we suddenly looked out of date. **"**
> **– Meg Bishop, product manager**

Could technological change in the next three years affect your organisation? If you suddenly faced a massive change in your business, how would it affect your company? Do you have a strategy which will prepare you for it?

Being PEST-aware isn't a matter of feeling depressed about the things outside of your control that can go wrong. It's simply a way of discovering the truth in the adage that "forewarned is forearmed".

Primary research

This involves getting data specially created for your purposes. It takes quite a bit more time, effort and money to lay your hands on but, in the end, you will have the information you *really* want. The most common source of primary data is the sample questionnaire given to existing or potential clients. Designing an effective questionnaire is an art. It is very important to avoid asking leading questions or ones that encourage the participant to give the answers you want. Here are some rule-of-thumb guidelines for creating a market research questionnaire.

○ *Once again, you must decide what exactly you need to know. In addition to full personal details, you may want to know about: where your market exists, what products or services the market is looking for, what price the customer is willing to pay and so on.*
○ *Avoid vague generalisations, such as "do you like our product?" or "what type of service would you like to see from us?"*
○ *Make sure it suits the method you intend to use to conduct your survey – i.e. by face-to-face interview, telephone, mail, fax or e-mail.*
○ *Find out as much as you can about the attitudes of existing or potential customers. Ask about: satisfaction with existing products, the strengths and weaknesses of existing products, product improvements that would be welcome, opportunities for new product developments, and how the customer makes purchasing decisions*
○ *Make sure that your finding are measurable – i.e. that you can quantify the responses and make decisions that are truly founded on your customers' views.*

❝ *In our first customer survey, we asked "What do you think about our product?" We got 171 "OK"s, 366 "nice", 12 "very nice" and so on. We soon learnt to give the respondents measurable options, such as rating on a scale of 1 to 5 how much they liked our existing products.* ❞
– Barry Brown, product development consultant

The more you know about your customers' buying habits the better. It's also a good idea to find out what they think are your strengths and weaknesses.

> When you see customer service questionnaires, do you wonder "why do they want to know" and "how will it help their marketing strategy"?

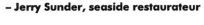

66 The beauty of these questionnaires is that the very act of giving them out is a good marketing opportunity. You're telling the customer "we really care about your views and service really matters to us." That can be very important in a business that relies on repeat trade and reputation. 99
– Jerry Sunder, seaside restaurateur

> Design a simple questionnaire that you could put to your customers. How would you make sure every customer saw it, each form was read, and that every completed form was collected?

Analysing your findings

Once you have completed your market research, it is time to evaluate and analyse your findings. You should focus your analysis on two main questions:

○ *How can we improve sales of our existing products?*
○ *How can we expand into new markets?*

Grade your findings into low, medium and high potential. Concentrate your efforts and resources on the high potential areas – at least to start with.

Simple ways to get to know your customers' needs

1. Persuade yourself and your colleagues that market research is worth while.
2. Ask yourself: "What do we need to know about our business in order to improve customer satisfaction?"
3. Clarify your aims and objectives, and think how best to achieve the desired results. Set aside time to devise a customer survey which will help you get the right results.
4. Decide whether you need to do primary or secondary research (or both) to satisfy your market research needs.
5. Find out what sources of secondary information are available – your local reference library is a good place to start.
6. Carry out an internal marketing audit of your current business to identify growth areas and weaknesses.
7. Carry out a PEST analysis to assess how you might be affected by changes in the Political climate, Economic conditions, Social trends and Technological developments.
8. Start reading the business press more carefully – this is a good place to look for trends that are going to affect you.
9. Once you've got the information about your customers (existing and potential), analyse the results and look for ways to improve the way you do business with them.

What's in this chapter for you

What's the marketing mix got to do with me?
Five stages in getting your product right
The product life cycle
Setting the price and positioning
Making products less price sensitive
Unique selling points (USPs)

❝ *Marketing costs money and takes time – it's essential we get the right marketing mix for our products.* ❞
– Anne Cameron, stationers' marketing manager

What's the marketing mix got to do with me?

"Marketing Mix" – you will undoubtedly have heard this common piece of marketing-speak. In fact it is quite a useful little expression that sums up a lot about marketing decisions. As we have already said, marketing is not about changing one factor at a time to come up with some magic formula that will increase your sales. It involves a process – a series of decisions about the four key Ps of marketing: Product, Price, Place and Promotion: "OK let's alter price but at the same time change the product a little, sell into a new market and do our best to promote it."

The marketing mix, then, is simply how you juggle these 4Ps to get the greatest customer satisfaction – and, for you, that means **profit**!

Making decisions about your PRODUCT

It is worth reiterating that by the word "product" we mean both goods and services – anything your business or organisation produces or does that is in some way traded.

Take a moment to think about your product/s. How long has your company been producing this product? How long will it go on producing it do you think? How will the product change and develop?

The most difficult decision any business has to make involves asking "What do we produce, and is it still the right choice?" The most obvious reason for product failure is to misunderstand the market – in other words to misread what the customers will buy and how much they will pay. The business world is littered with great ideas that never took off.

> **66** *If the customers' wishes are not taken into account, or wrongly interpreted, failure will not be far behind.* **99**
> **Sharon Ball, publisher**

So, you need to identify your customers' needs – but how? This goes back to asking "Who are our customers?" Are you sure, for example, that the person who buys your product is the person who *uses* it? In many cases the customer is not just the person who buys it – think about family cars or television sets. In the latter case, the most important customer may be the children in a family.

Don't forget *potential* customers – those waiting out there who would be willing to buy your product but you haven't got to them yet. Perhaps you haven't identified who they are or you are trying to sell them the wrong product.

> **Take a moment to think about who your customers really are. Assuming that you have identified your customers correctly, how can you be sure that your product satisfies their needs? Do you know what their needs are? They are likely to be more complex than you think.**

Take the example of a motor car: think about the needs of potential car buyers. The obvious answer is they want to get from A to B. But there other important needs that should be satisfied: the need to be economical, the need for the car to look good, the need to make the drivers and passengers feel good.

Why are these customers buying your product? Again, simple market research should answer this question. Ask customers directly (but politely) and/or add a section in your customer feedback form about why they bought the product and how they intend to use it.

Identify your product and capability

In thinking about your product there is one extremely important bit of marketing jargon that will be really invaluable to you: **The Product Life Cycle.** We will come to that in detail later, in the meantime think about why you are producing/selling your current range of products. Be wary of saying "It's what we've always been known for" or "We can't do anything else". If you answer "This is almost a hobby for us" you may have developed an unhealthy producer orientation rather than being customer focused.

| What would you say about the reasons why you make your current product? Any of the above? Be honest. | |

Many businesses have gone under by producing the wrong things for the wrong reasons. Remember the core of marketing: keep the customer forever in your sights. Are you doing everything for and only for the customer? There is little room for sentiment or habit in the choice of products.

Assuming that you know what your customers really want, do you have the capacity to meet their needs? If your answer is "Yes, I know the way the market is going, but no, we can't meet that need" then you are accepting defeat. One way forward is to carry out a thorough SWOT analysis across the business. SWOT simply stands for:

○ *Strengths*
○ *Weaknesses*
○ *Opportunities*
○ *Threats*.

Ask your colleagues to spend some time discussing these four issues. It can be an extremely powerful means of talking over problems that otherwise do not come to light. It can also be an excellent forum for new ideas. Every business should carry out a SWOT exercise – make sure that you involve the whole workforce.

Let's look at the example of Premier Printers, a local jobbing print firm.

> ○ **Strengths** – good local reputation, motivated workforce, good customer network, rapid delivery, healthy balance sheet.
> ○ **Weaknesses** – reliance on traditional products such as fliers, leaflets, brochures.
> ○ **Opportunities** – contract work with local college, photocopying and fax services, business stationery.
> ○ **Threats** – home desk-top publishing, increasing local competition, coming recession.

After the SWOT exercise, the boss of Premier Printers decided to run down their traditional business and build up the more specialised side. Investment in equipment and training was approved.

What would you list in a SWOT analysis of your business operation?

Match your customers' needs to your capability

This can be done on a fairly simple level:

> ○ *(1) Identify the features of your product – in other words, what does your product do?*
> ○ *(2) Identify how customers benefit from these features – this is what the customers need.*
> ○ *(3) Think about customer needs that are not met by your product's features.*
> ○ *(4) Think about how new products could be developed by your business which would meet customer needs better.*

Your product now and in the future

> **❝** We had been offering the same service to tourists for about 15 years. Our cottages had always seemed popular and bookings were steady. We just didn't see that the market was changing and before we knew it, we were selling two-week holidays that no one seemed to want any more.**❞**
> **– Brian Mitchell, caravan and cottage holidays**

> Are you making the right product for now and the future? Can you afford to sit back on past successes? The answer in both cases is likely to be "no".

In this highly competitive world, no one (least of all the small or medium-sized business) can afford to be complacent about the product he or she brings to the market-place.

One useful way of thinking about your product's position is the product life cycle, a vital tool to get you thinking about your product – its present and, more importantly, its future.

Product life cycle

This is bound up with such questions as:

○ *Should we invest more in this product?*
○ *Should we promote this product more actively?*
○ *Should we start to adapt and change our product?*
○ *Is our product going to stop selling?*

These questions and more are addressed by the product life cycle. Businesses only thrive if the products they put on the market match the needs of customers. But these needs keep changing – what was wildly popular this year may be on its way out next year. The product life cycle can help you make solid judgements about the present and future for your product.

However great it is, no product lives for ever. A product's life cycle is made up of four stages:

○ *Launch*
○ *Growth*
○ *Maturity*
○ *Decline.*

All products seem to follow this cycle. It is a very sensible idea to know where your product is on this cycle – if, for instance, it is just about to enter the decline phase, you should think twice about pouring advertising funds into promoting it.

Let's take each phase in turn – and think about your own product(s) as each stage is explained.

Launch

This is a very tense time. Giving birth to a new product can be a painful and sometimes tragic process. The infant mortality of new products is alarmingly high – some say that only 20 per cent of new products survive.

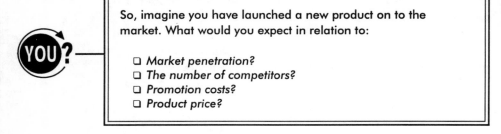

So, imagine you have launched a new product on to the market. What would you expect in relation to:

❏ *Market penetration?*
❏ *The number of competitors?*
❏ *Promotion costs?*
❏ *Product price?*

In most cases, but not all, the launch phase tends to mean that market penetration is low – the product has not had time to make an impact. Depending on the product, there may be relatively few competitors, especially if the product is breaking new ground. The cost of promoting the product will be high, especially in terms of unit promotion costs. (Why? Because the overhead promotion costs are matched by relatively low initial sales. It may well be that your existing products will have to carry the newcomer until it is more established.) Price is typically high at the launch of a new product – it is much more sensible to start with a high price and bring it down later than the other way round.

In this early phase the product may be more strongly differentiated from other products – in other words, your competitors haven't had time to imitate the product. In this phase the growth of sales is relatively slow. It takes time to get established.

Growth

If your product has survived the launch phase, it is likely that it will enter a growth phase. Now sales are starting to accelerate as the product is becoming well established. Typical characteristics of the growth phase are:

○ *Sales trends up*
○ *Competitors start to imitate and new rivals start to emerge*

- *Promotion costs remain high but unit costs start to fall*
- *The product is using up a large proportion of management time and other resources*
- *The product may adapt or move into specialist niche markets.*

Maturity

Sales are still rising as the product continues to win market share, but the growth rate has definitely slowed down. The product has now reached a critical stage.

- *Much of the market has now been penetrated*
- *Promotional support is lower – the product is now well known*
- *Prices are more established and stable.*

You will have to live with competitors (unless you have a patent or some other device to protect your product). But, looking on the bright side, this is a good sign – it means that there really is a market out there for your product.

How can this maturity stage be prolonged? One common way is to develop a strong brand image for your product. Think of strong brands such as Heinz Baked Beans, Coca-Cola, Levis Jeans. They have all carved out a strong niche in the market and it is very difficult for rivals to dent their market share. Can you do the same?

A new brand image may give an old product new life and indeed it may enter a product life cycle of its own starting with the brand launch. However, developing a brand is an expensive business and will require a heavy commitment to promotional funds.

Decline

All good things must come to an end! There will come a time when even the strongest products start to lose market share – indeed sales will start to decline. This is a very dangerous time. Many companies are so close to their products that they don't recognise that the decline phase has started. They cling to the old products, tying up scarce resources behind "yesterday's breadwinners".

❝ Our flagship publication was a directory started up by the company founder. It was a nightmare to put together but we ploughed money into it year after year, jazzing up the design and using fancy binding to try to avert the slumping sales. Then somebody found out that virtually all of the data we used was available for free on the internet! It was time to abandon tradition or face disaster. ❞

– Sharon Ball

How long will it take for our product to reach decline? This is impossible to say – each product is different. What is important is to keep a close eye on where you are in the cycle. Watch for the signs. Here are some typical characteristics of the decline phase:

- *The number of rival products is starting to decline*
- *Rivals are bringing out new products*
- *Sales are falling and there may be a need for considerable price discounting to keep it alive.*

Do not get caught out in this phase by throwing a lot of resources into a product that has reached the end of its life.

Think about the product life cycle. At which stages are your product(s)? Are you sure you are making the right decisions about price, the sales effort, promotion, investment in resources, and management time? If you think you're making the wrong decisions, now is the time to reassess your approach.

So, what can be done to take the product life cycle into account when marketing your products?

Some practical tips to keep your product alive

- ❑ *Make sure that your product is clearly differentiated from others in the market.*
- ❑ *Think about developing a clearer brand image.*
- ❑ *Keep in close touch with customers – what are their current tastes and needs, what do they think about your product? Listen to the people most active in making your sales.*

❑ *Maintain standards at all times – invest if necessary in staff training and make sure that everyone is motivated and thoroughly supporting the product.*
❑ *Keep checking on where you are on the product life cycle and discuss this regularly with colleagues.*

Setting the PRICE

Price is the second of the 4Ps of marketing. Assuming that you have a product to sell, the next question is: "How will you decide on the price?" It is tempting to see price merely as an accounting solution or part of a cost equation.

> ❝ *We always stick to a rigid price formula of multiplying the unit cost by 2.2 and then add VAT.* ❞
> **– Al Hobson, souvenir wholesaler**

Seeing price as a passive add-on to unit costs can be a very dangerous move. Do not leave price decisions to the accountants or simply use the result of some fixed formula.

Price is part of the marketing mix. It is just as much part of the marketing strategy as the product launch or promotions. Price, of course, has to cover costs, but the determination of price should primarily be a marketing decision. Getting the price decision wrong can be a very public mistake. The wrong price can kill the best product.

> ❝ *Pricing must take the customer into account. The price he or she pays is a measure of the value placed on your product.* ❞
> **– Frank Ramsey, market gardener**

The right price matches the customer's assessment of the balance between sacrifice (payment) and the benefit gained. A high-price and low-quality product is obviously the worst combination.

What price can I charge?

Experience has shown that customers have a "price expectation" for products. They make a subconscious calculation of the benefits to them of a product and that determines how much they are prepared to pay for it. This is their "expected price". It is a calculation based on their perception of "value for money".

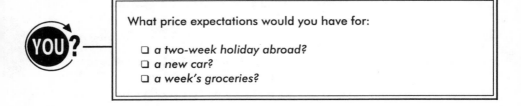

> **What price expectations would you have for:**
>
> ❑ a two-week holiday abroad?
> ❑ a new car?
> ❑ a week's groceries?

In many markets, customers are relatively indifferent to price changes within a certain tolerance range around the expected price. For some products this range may be low (say, 5 per cent either way) or in other products, the range could be high (e.g. plus or minus 20 per cent).

This idea can be expressed in terms of price sensitivity. Price sensitive products are those for which customers are intolerant of price increases. A small rise in price may lead to a much larger fall in sales. This would obviously be bad news for the producer.

Making products less price sensitive

Here's how to make your products less price sensitive. Make sure that the product is:

○ *highly differentiated from others – i.e. that it has a "unique selling point" (see below)*
○ *seen as a high-quality product with few rivals – this quality mark could be associated with the product's features and/or the service you provide.*

Positioning

This is a matter of how your product is perceived in the market. Your product can be placed in any one of nine different categories, as shown in the matrix below.

Least value	Poor value	Best of class
Poor value	Average value	High value
Cheap & nasty	Cheap & cheerful	Super value

Note that quality increases as you go from left to right and price decreases from top to bottom. Hence, the top right-hand cell ("best of class") represents a high-quality product at a high price. At the other extreme, "cheap & nasty" includes products which are low quality and low price.

○ *You should regard the shaded sectors as no-go areas. Here you are only offering poor value and you'll find your customers voting with their feet.*

○ *You might be tempted to place your product in the "average value" sector (mid-price, mid-quality) but remember that, in this position, you will be highly vulnerable to competition from products positioned in the "high" and "super" value sectors as well from "cheap & cheerful" products.*

○ *The "cheap & cheerful" category (reasonable quality at a low price) can be attractive if you are going for a mass market. Although this is often a successful strategy, bear in mind that such products are highly price sensitive and open to fierce competition. Also, you may find that your margins are so low that market downturns could spell disaster.*

○ *If you are in the "best of class" segment, price sensitivity will not be a problem – quality is more important than price. Make sure your product is truly as great as you think it is.*

Remember that, for the customer, price is an indicator of quality. Is your price strategy sending the right messages? Look back at the matrix and answer some crucial questions:

❑ *Where are you now and where should you be?*

❑ *Should you reposition your product and, therefore, your price?*

❑ *Are some of your customers more price sensitive than others? If so, can you identify them and adjust your prices in only those segments of the market?*

Remember: Price is a marketing decision.

Unique selling points (USPs)

One important way to differentiate your product is to give it a "unique selling point". A USP could be any of the following qualities:

- ○ **For products:** *the range you offer, the availability, price and value for money, design and packaging, reliability, and after-sales service.*
- ○ **For services:** *your experience and reputation, a list of satisfied customers willing to endorse your work, your network of contacts, and so on . . .*

    ❝ *At first we couldn't think of any USPs for our products – after all, a pizza is a pizza. But we put some more thought in, asked our customers and spied on our rivals, and then came up with quite a few. Not least was our range of toppings and side orders, then our free delivery service and prices next to lowest. Add to this the fact that you always get your pizza with a smile, and there it is – our USPs.* ❞
– Fran Cutter, Pronto Pizzas

How to get your product and price right

1. Think the unthinkable – your product might not be all it should. Do not cling to the past ways of doing things and stick with products because they are "part of the furniture".
2. Identify your products and where they are heading. Ensure your capabilities are adequate to satisfy the market.
3. Look at the list of customer needs against your capabilities and identify any gaps.
4. Carry out a SWOT analysis on your whole organisation to assess your Strengths and Weaknesses, Opportunities and Threats.
5. Draw up a product life cycle for your activities – where are you now and where will you be in one, three and five years' time.

6. If your product is in decline use branding to keep it alive – household names enjoy a much longer life expectancy.

7. Make sure your pricing decisions are based on marketing considerations and not formulaic number crunching.

8. Take whatever action you can to reduce the price sensitivity of your product by emphasising quality issues.

9. Re-position your product if it becomes clear you are wasting resources by competing in the wrong market segment.

What's in this chapter for you

Place: getting goods to the right place at the right time
Promotion: creating awareness of your product
Tips on promotional tools
How to manage your own public relations
Promotion planning

❝ *Why are we here? My grandfather started the business here 60 years ago and we've never moved.* ❞
– Paula Foss, caterer

PLACE: Getting goods to the right place at the right time

The third P in the marketing mix is all about which channels to use both for the physical distribution and selling of the product, the relevant costs and benefits of those channels, and the feasibility of using the different channels.

What are your options? If you are a relatively small manufacturer you may, for example, sell your product range directly to the customer via mail order or retail outlet. You may decide to sell via a mix of channels, such as a sales force, commission agents, wholesalers, direct response advertising, mail order houses, department stores, multiple store groups, small retailers.

If you are selling a service, it's likely that you need to be near your customers.

Making decisions about Place

❝ *We moved here because this is where the majority of our customers live and our products incur a large distribution cost.* ❞
– Bill Kennedy, piano dealer

Decisions about place are based on the answers to the following questions:

○ *Where are your customers?*
○ *Do you need to be close to your customers?*
○ *Do they require after-sales service?*
○ *Do they need you to provide face-to-face service?*

○ *How significant is the distribution cost of getting your product to your customers?*

❝ *We sell and distribute almost exclusively via the net and by post so our customers can be anywhere in the world.* ❞
– Barbara Taylor, stamps and collectables

Accessibility is the most important feature for your customer. This doesn't mean you have to be physically near to them. For old and disabled customers, you may need to have good mail order and delivery systems. Many businesses are now selling goods and services via the internet. Accessibility is only a matter of having a web site that can be easily and quickly found.

Ask yourself: "Are we really located in the right place?" "Do our customers demand that we be in a different place – more accessible?"

If your customers are very widely spread and you cannot afford to distribute to them direct, consider using the services of a wholesaler.

Remember: Place decisions should aim at:

❏ *making the product readily available where it is needed when it is needed, or*
❏ *getting the product to the right place at the right time, which means getting your distribution channels right.*

Assess your distribution channels continuously, both from the perspective of your own costs and in the interest of your customers. Check out the alternatives – it is always worth looking at the costs and benefits of choosing another option.

Promotion: creating awareness of your product

This is the final P in the marketing mix. Promotion involves *informing* people about your organisation and products, and *persuading* them that they should come to you, not your competitors.

Many people think this is all to do with advertising but a lot of businesses have an effective promotions programme without spending anything on advertising. Advertising is just one means of promoting your product – there are other ways of making customers aware that your product exists and what benefits it offers.

What promotional tools are available?

The most common techniques used in promotional processes are:

- ○ *Impersonal tools – promotion at a distance, such as the signs on shop windows, the paintwork on company vehicles or an internet site.*
- ○ *Advertising – this can be very expensive, depending on the media chosen, and should only be done after careful research and thought.*
- ○ *Direct mail – can be very effective for a wide range of products (see the following chapter).*
- ○ *Public relations – can be a very cheap and effective way of getting exposure for your product, but things can go wrong.*
- ○ *Promotional literature – these days, almost an essential expenditure. Make sure it is up to date, says everything you want, and gives the right image.*

Are you accounting for any money spent on advertising? Could the money be better spent?

❝ *I did a quick survey and found that only the over 50s tend to read our local freebie newspaper. No wonder we weren't getting much response.* ❞
– Sal Greenway, children's party organiser

When we think of promotion we tend to think of advertising. It can be very effective but it is also very expensive (or can be). Think carefully before continuing to spend on advertising (or starting for the first time).

> Check that you are getting good value for money from your advertising budget.
>
> ❑ *How many readers (or viewers) see your advertisement?*
> ❑ *How many of these make a sales enquiry?*
> ❑ *How many of these are turned into sales?*
> ❑ *What would happen if you stopped advertising for a time?*
> ❑ *Are you targeting your advertising properly – i.e. is it being read or seen by potential customers? If not, what other media would be more suitable?*

> ❝ *We used to throw good money at fancy ads placed in the Sunday national press – some of our rivals did, so we followed suit. One month we decided to see what happened if we stopped the ads. The answer was, not much. Since then, we have targeted our advertising budget on where we think our potential buyers are: some trade journals, special interest mags and club newsletters (very cheap).* ❞
> **– Bert Morris, camping equipment business**

To the list of tools above, we must add personal tools. These involve face-to-face promotion techniques, such as door-to-door interviewing, talking to customers in retail outlets or taking a trade stand at exhibitions.

Each tool has different strengths and weaknesses. The trick is to select the right ones to achieve your marketing objectives in a cost-effective way. When choosing which tools to use, remember that your promotional effort should do the four things summed up by the acronym "AIDA":

○ attract **A**ttention
○ arouse **I**nterest
○ create **D**esire
○ prompt **A**ction.

> How are your products promoted at present – which tools are used and why? Does each tool meet the AIDA targets?

❝ We have excellent relations with our local newspaper and several trade journals. If we have a story to tell, we write a press release and send a photo – they usually print it and it's great free publicity. ❞
– Jan Hall, safety planning consultant

How to manage your own public relations (PR)

Public relations is often the forgotten side of marketing. People think it's very up-market or that you need some specialist department or expensive consultants. In fact, you can do most of it yourself. Here's how.

(1) Journalists love a story and editors hate empty spaces. Make contact with some useful journalists who can help promote your product. Send them newsy stories and photographs that will interest their readers.

(2) No news? Create some. For starters, you can have celebrations of special events: "Pimple-fest after five years of Chocolate Making" or "Anyfirm welcomes its 100th customer with a grand prize".

(3) Sponsor a local event – a school fete, a sports day, a local junior league. This will always get you good coverage (and will do wonders for your sense of community).

(4) Get yourself invited on to local radio by offering to speak as an expert in your field. They are always looking for people to interview.

(5) Send regular press releases and articles to specialist magazines that your customers tend to read – it isn't all that hard and specialist journals are always looking for a short, interesting article.

The key to writing great copy

Follow these simple rules and you will soon be producing copy that the press love to print.

○ *Start with a bang. Say all you have to say in the first sentence:*
   "Goddards have won a huge contract for drilling"
   "Joe Soap Ltd is first in the region to sell Albanian wine"
○ *Remember WWW. The story must tell you:*
   What happened
   When it happened
   Who was involved

○ *Try to include one quote (and do a bit of subtle selling):*
With the arrival of 200 bottles of Tirana Red, Joe Soap has become the first firm in the area to sell Albanian wine. "We are very proud to take the lead in this exciting new product – it tastes great and should be very popular," enthused Joe.

○ *Keep it short and simple*
A press release should not run to more than one page. Keep it down to around 250–300 words.

It takes practice to perfect the art of putting together an arresting press release but the benefits will more than re-pay the effort. Write and then re-write, cutting and refining each time, until you are sure it will arouse interest and create excitement about your product.

Promotion Planning

> ❝ *We don't spend a penny on advertising but we do sponsor local events, including a football league, and we make sure we're associated with most things that go on in this town* ❞
> **– Reg Rogan, sportswear retailer**

Before you spend anything on promotion, you should plan your strategy very carefully. The best place to start is to look at what the successful competition does. How do they promote themselves? What image do they send? What is their USP – can you be better?

Once you have a clear idea what others are doing, go through the following process:

❑ *Identify your target market carefully. What characteristics does it have?*

❑ *Decide who you are aiming your promotion at – i.e. who are the decision-makers?*

❑ *Refine the message you want to send to them.*

❑ *Assess which is likely to be the most effective medium to carry your message and reach the decision-makers. Brochures? Advertising? Direct mail? Radio and television?*

❑ *Decide which is the best time to promote your organisation.*

Remember: Promotion is everybody's business, even if you never meet the customer face to face. Promotion can seriously boost your organisation's image so it's well worth getting it right and planning is the key to this.

How to make good **Place and Promotion** decisions

1. Review your Place decision – does it still make sense? Where does the customer want you to be?
2. Can you make savings on distribution and still meet customer expectations by moving to another location?
3. Review your advertising budget regularly and very critically – is every advertisement paying its way?
4. Check that the image of your promotional literature is right. It will not be a waste of money to commission a professional designer to help you.
5. Check that all your literature is up to date and that it conveys the message you want it to.
6. Ask yourself if audio-visual presentations, trade stands or personal contacts might be more effective than promotional literature alone.
7. Check each of your promotional methods against the AIDA criteria – are they attracting Attention, arousing Interest, creating Desire and prompting Action?
8. Consider how you can develop better public relations. Could you use celebrity openings and demonstrations to further your aims?
9. Start making contacts with useful journalists who would be willing to use your expertise in your area of business.
10. Draw up a promotion planning strategy to guide you towards the best possible means of promoting your business and to keep you where you want to be.

Marketing isn't about using one tool at a time but balancing each of the 4Ps to maximum effect – literally trying to get the right mix of marketing tools. You cannot afford to ignore it because marketing means customers and customers mean profits and survival. Marketing should be a continuous process that everyone in the business is involved in.

What's in this chapter for you

The pros and cons of direct mail
Understanding the market
Setting your objectives
Mailing lists

❝ *We used to send 2000 mail shots a day. We then did a bit of a survey of recipients and found that over 60 per cent of letters were sifted by PAs and most never got as far as the decision-makers.* ❞
– June Summers, Gift Express

The pros and cons of direct mail

Direct mail tends to have a bad name. We have all been irritated by the mass of "junk mail" coming every day. But it needn't be like that.

What do you think about the direct mail shots you receive? Here is a typical view: "Junk mail is stuff sent to the wrong person – it's anonymous." This is often true.

Direct mail can be very effective if it has the right message and is sent to the most appropriate customers. "Junk mail" is that which has no addressee – "Dear Customer" or "Dear Occupant". Good direct mail is properly addressed and gets to the right person. This takes some planning. The benefits of good direct mail are:

○ *It is very flexible and can target specific customers in each market segment. You can, of course, even target specific, named people.*
○ *You can time your promotion exactly to suit your production or service plans.*
○ *You can enclose reply cards that help to get you instant marketing feedback and good leads.*
○ *You can keep close control of costs by monitoring the response rate.*

So, what are the disadvantages of direct mail?

○ There are lots of rules and regulations you need to understand to know what you can and cannot say or offer in the post.
○ You need to spend time and money building up a good mailing list to target actual decision-makers.
○ You need good design skills to give your mail shot the right image and get your message over effectively (although you can hire the necessary help).

> **❝** *One company keeps sending me its product list – not that I've ever asked for it – produced on two sides of A4 paper, single spaced and in a horrible, illegible font that you can't read. Whenever I see their envelope, I put it straight in the bin.* **❞**
> **– Terry Bathurst, engineer**

Understanding the market

Direct mail can be amazingly effective, but it isn't cheap. Consequently, it's important that you plan your direct mail strategy very carefully. The first stage is to really understand your market.

Look at your market:

❑ *Put together a detailed profile of your customers. Find out about their buying habits and anything you can about changing tastes.*
❑ *Ask what your customers think of you and your organisation.*
❑ *What does the competition do? Start collecting some of their direct mail. It's easy to do this – just get on their mailing list or ring them and ask for details. Think of ways how you can improve on what they do.*
❑ *Draw up a list of pros and cons of using direct mail to reach customers in your market.*

If you feel direct mail will work for you, there are some preliminary steps which should be taken. Join a relevant trade organisation and find out about what rules and regulations they have about direct mail. Talk to printers about direct mail jobs they handle. What seems to be working well these days? What type of direct mail printing do their customers keep asking for?

It's also worth test running a version of your mail shot on

existing customers (even friends and relatives). Ask them for a critical opinion of its design, layout, message and timing.

Setting your objectives

Once you have committed yourself to a direct mail campaign, you need to start the detailed planning and costing for it. The first stage is to think about your direct mail budget.

> 66 *We started direct mail last year and now find it a really powerful tool. But, at first, we wasted a lot of money on poorly designed stuff that nobody would really want to read. It was too wordy and boring.*
> 99
> **– Jill Lewis, pottery company owner**

Here are some useful costing tips

Quotes: Get several quotes for your stationery. It is likely to be much cheaper if bought in bulk. Try the mail order stationery firms but don't forget your local suppliers and printers. You may be able to do a deal with them that includes everything you need – paper, envelopes, specialist papers and film, folding, packing and printing.

Ask lots of printers – prices vary enormously but beware of long lead times, "hidden costs" of making amendments and additions, delivery charges, quality of papers used and so on. If it's your first time, start small but remember that unit print costs fall dramatically with increased volume.

Budgeting: Make sure that you don't overlook any expenses. You will need to cover the costs of:

- *buying or researching the mailing lists*
- *designing and printing the mail shots (including all materials)*
- *postage and packing – do a test weighing to calculate the costs of each posting*
- *using a franking machine service if you intend to post many per day*
- *all the time it is going to take to get the campaign up and running*
- *extra help you may need for posting, packing, sorting and so on.*

Before you embark on direct mailing, you should ask yourself some important questions:

What do you want to achieve by using direct mail? Think in measurable terms:

- ❑ *the number of responses and enquiries generated*
- ❑ *the number of promising leads and appointments*
- ❑ *direct sales*
- ❑ *additions to your mailing list.*

With the short-term objectives set and costed, think also about the medium and long term. Where, for instance, could direct mail take you in one, three or five years?

Mailing lists

You can't use direct mail unless you have an addressee – and you need to get to the right person.

> ❝ *In our experience, it's little use sending your mail to 'The Managing Director' or 'The person in charge of buying'. It is likely to go straight into the bin.* ❞
>
> **– Jill Lewis**

So, where do you get a worthwhile mailing list? The cheapest way (and often the best if you have the time and commitment) is to build up your own. Start with people you know – your existing customers (it is very important to keep comprehensive and up-to-date information about them).

Do you keep good customer records on file or in a computer database? Are they regularly and systematically updated? If not, they should be.

Also try tapping contacts, friends and friends of friends. Self-generated mailing lists are much more likely to generate good leads than ones bought off the shelf.

Scour the free sources of mailing info. These include the business pages of the telephone directory, Yellow Pages, Top 1000 Companies (try the business section of your local library), membership lists of trade organisations (often readily available for a very small charge), members of the local chambers of commerce, business clubs, small firm associations, institutes, federations and so on.

Once you have addresses, get some names of decision-makers. The telephone is very useful here and organisations are usually happy to give you the details of the people you need (see the section on telemarketing for more on this).

If you do not have the resources to put together your own mailing list, consider renting or buying one from a specialist commercial organisation. There are many such organisations that provide contact names and addresses. Seek out specialist magazines where mailing list providers advertise their services.

Here are some guidelines for buying into useful mailing lists:

- ❑ *Always buy lists from reputable companies – preferably those which belong to a trade association.*
- ❑ *Before you buy, make sure the list is accurate and up to date. Ask what come-back you have if it proves to be otherwise. Ask for a sample so you can test out the accuracy of the details.*
- ❑ *Before you print out any mailing list on to labels, check it over to make sure it is what you want and that there aren't any obvious errors, duplications or irrelevant addresses.*

❝ *The most common error is one name appearing several times – maybe in full, then with one initial, then with two. I know from experience that it can be very irritating to get the same mail shot four or five times over.* ❞

– Jill Lewis

Make sure you spend time updating the lists once you have them. People and addresses change quickly – check the details every three months or so. Also, make sure you keep records of all mailings sent and any enquiries or other responses you get. There are several excellent software packages which can help you keep track of customer data.

It is vital to ensure that you comply with national and international data protection legislation. In the UK, the Data Protection Act of 1984 requires anyone who holds computerised records on people to register these with the Data Protection Register. Once registered, you must comply with the standards set. For most organisations this is simply a matter of common sense – acting in a fair and open manner, allowing full access, complying with rules on disclosure to third parties and so on.

Ways to get the best from direct mail

1. Plan very carefully what you want to send – add reply cards, coupons and other methods that encourage customers to reply (even if to say "no"). Use a professional designer to give you something seriously eye-catching.

2. Wherever possible, include a personalised letter that uses the customer's name. Always direct your shot at the decision-makers.

3. Start collecting direct mail sent by competitors – learn from them and think of ways it could be done better.

4. The costs of direct mail can quickly spiral upwards so make a detailed budget for all aspects of the mailing.

5. Draw up a careful plan of campaign – Who will you be targeting? What are you offering? Test out the mailing on friends and a trial number of customers.

6. Put together your own mailing list – from what and who you already know, and from your own research. The simplest form of mailing list is to enter names and addresses of potential (or existing) customers on to a mail merge program – they come with most wordprocessing packages. They can then be merged into an existing letter or template document. It's really easy once you start.

7. If you are selling to business customers, spend an hour or so in the commercial library – using directories, year books, journals and telephone directories. This way, you can put together a relevant mailing list quickly (at least company names and addresses).

8. Shop around for commercial mailing lists and ask for a trial sample to check for accuracy.

9. Check your lists before using them and always build in regular maintenance time.

What's in this chapter for you

Five compelling reasons for doing it by phone
Getting appointments
Knowing what to say and do

> **❝** *I've tried all forms of marketing, and believe me,*
> *telemarketing is, without doubt, the most effective and instant form.*
> *Its success rates are far higher than direct mail or other forms of*
> *marketing in my business.* **❞**
> **– Mike Ramsay, Direct Marketing Concepts**

Five compelling reasons for doing it by phone

Marketing your product on the telephone can be a very effective
way of getting results. Mike certainly believes that the response rate is
many times higher than with direct mail or other forms of marketing.

Look at the five major strengths of telemarketing:

❑ First, you get straight to the decision-maker. Most mail is
  filtered by secretaries, assistants and PAs. Using the
  telephone helps you get past the "gatekeepers".
❑ Second, it's a two-way medium – you can judge the
  response to your product from the tone and content of the
  other person's replies. You can also talk to the reception
  staff and find out more about the people you need to speak
  to, their position, influence and so on.
❑ Third, the telephone is a powerful means of
  communication – used correctly, it can be very persuasive.
  You can use all your skills as a sales person.
❑ Fourth, you can overcome objections and move towards
  your objectives (which may be an appointment or a sale).
❑ Fifth, you can establish a rapport and find out what the
  customer is thinking, what he or she needs from you.

> **❝** *I got a call the other day from a telemarketing guy*
> *who began his call, "I don't suppose you want to hear about our*
> *product but . . ." That's an instant invitation to put the phone*
> *down. You've got to be positive.* **❞**
> **– Mike Ramsay**

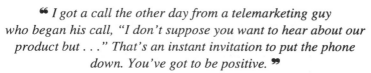

Getting the ring of confidence

How confident do you sound on the telephone? What telesales calls have impressed you?

Telemarketing is only as good as the person making the call. Not everyone is confident using the telephone – they get tongue-tied, nervous and sound unconvincing or apologetic. People hired to make the calls are often young, inexperienced and have simply been given a script to read without any training.

> ❝ *Whenever I hear those callow voices sounding like automatons, I say, "I'm dead busy at the moment but I've got your number so I'll call you right back," and put the phone down!* ❞
> **– Carol Jenkins, PA**

Does Carol's reaction sound familiar? Here are some tips from the professionals.

Some easy ways to improve your telemarketing skills

❑ *Marketing is the life blood of business. Whenever possible, make sure that a senior person makes the call. Callers should have the weight of their organisation behind them.*
    Which would impress you more: "Hello, I'm calling on behalf of ABC Supplies who are just starting their annual sale" or "Good morning, I'm Sheila Lee, Marketing Manager of ABC Supplies . . . "?

❑ *Introduce yourself using your name and title and make a note of the customer's name and position. If it's appropriate, try to establish a rapport by using the customer's Christian name as soon as possible.*

❑ *Try standing up when you make the call to help you feel important and in control.*

❑ *Imagine that you are paying a personal call to the customer. It's important that you feel this is part of customer care and not just any old phone call.*

❑ *Use notes by all means, but never stick to a prepared script. Notes should only be used as a memory jogger.*

❑ *Most people respond to a touch of humour and a pleasant, friendly and confident voice. Ask colleagues to assess your telephone manner (it may not be what you think) and work on any weaknesses. Try to eliminate too many pauses, or 'um's and 'aah's. You believe in your product – sound as if you do!*

Getting appointments

You may use the telephone to make a sale, but it is more likely to be effective as a means of getting to see your potential customer face to face.

> **❝** *Once I've got an appointment by telephone, I'm pretty sure of closing a sale.* **❞**
> **– Diane Lipple, sales manager for flooring company**

If getting an appointment is your goal, you have to work towards it – don't start your call with "Hello, can I come to see you about our product?" The answer is likely to be short and disappointing. Here are some golden rules from the experts.

How to get an appointment

❑ *Establish an early rapport with the customer with a polite and friendly introduction.*

❑ *Begin with a general overview of the product and its benefits and ask if now is the best time to talk about it. If not, arrange a time when the customer can talk to you over the telephone. Make a diary entry to ring at that time – and don't be late.*

❑ *Once you have the customer's attention, aim towards your goal – the appointment. Spend no more than five minutes outlining the advantages of the product and why it would suit the customer to see you face to face.*

❑ *Be prepared for objections such as:*
"I really don't think it's for us" – try countering with: "OK, can I send you some literature and discuss it with you another time?" The point here is to keep the lines of communication open.
"I'm not at liberty to make decisions right now" – you could ask: "Who should I talk to who can make these

decisions and when is the best time to ring back?"
"I'm not convinced" – you could say: "Look, it's best if I
can show you what we offer; can we fix a time to meet?"

If the customer's response is "I don't want it" and you end up putting the phone down, work on improving your selling skills. You should always know how to counter an objection (or interpret it). Your job as a sales person, is to listen and find ways to overcome the objections.

Always end a conversation amicably. It's right and proper to do so, but it may also help in future contacts.

Knowing what to say and do

There are no hard and fast rules about telemarketing. The main thing is to know what you want out of each telephone call – what are your objectives? As we have said, it is important to have a pleasant and easy manner on the telephone. This is especially true when talking to the gatekeepers.

> **❝** *I always like to establish a rapport with the receptionist or PA – the first person you're likely to speak to on the phone. Don't just say "Good morning, get me Mr Brown please." It's far better to spend a few seconds just making human contact: "Good morning, and what a cold one, my name's Di Lipple, Sales Manager of ABC. Could you possibly help me? Great! I need to speak to your buying department. Could you tell me who I should contact? Can you get her for me? Thanks very much.* **❞**
> — **Diane Lipple**

A word about fax and the internet

There is no doubt that modern technology is beginning to revolutionise the way we all do business. Faxes, and especially e-mails, can be sent quickly and very cheaply to anywhere in the world. But there are problems you should be aware of:

○ *Customers do not like receiving unsolicited fax messages or e-mails which take up their communications time.*
○ *Unsolicited faxes and e-mails have already gained a negative reputation.*

○ *You can't be sure who reads the faxes and e-mails.*
○ *The quality of the fax received may not be as good as you would wish it.*
○ *Faxes and e-mails don't always get the priority afforded to the post ("snail mail" still often gets more serious attention).*

Fax and e-mail is very useful where:

❑ *A customer has asked for information and needs it today.*
❑ *You need to send a long document or one with graphics and/or photographs (e-mail is especially useful for this).*
❑ *You need support for your documentation, or telemarketing call.*

The internet can also be used to create your own web sites. These can be accessed by anyone in the world (as long as they can find your internet address). These web sites can be very well designed using lots of colour, graphics – even sound and video. You can also incorporate reply boxes (via e-mail) and even add order forms using a credit card number. In this way, the internet can be used for direct sales – a kind of instant mail order.

Review your organisation's fax, e-mail and web site capability. Web site creation need not be expensive (though it may be costly to maintain).

Used properly, your phone lines can offer you an immensely powerful marketing tool.

Get the best out of your phone

1. Speak with authority but make friends with the reception staff and PAs (they are the vital gatekeepers en route to your customers).
2. Begin in a friendly, warm and assertive way – and get to the point quickly.

3. Have a writing pad or computer at the ready so that you can make notes of what the customer says, or any other contact information you glean.

4. Remember that telemarketing is selling – use your sales skills to the best of your ability. This means listening as well as speaking. Judge what the customer's needs are and be ready to meet them. Also be ready to counter objections.

5. Set your objectives clearly before the phone call – these may be: to send literature, to make an appointment, to send samples etc.

6. Smile when you speak, it will actually help you sound more relaxed and genuine.

7. Involve the customer at all times. Avoid hogging the phone. It's more important to listen to your customer than to talk at them.

8. Ask lots of questions to gauge the interests of your customer (and his or her ability to purchase your product).

9. Be bold – if you want a sale, make the close; if you want an appointment, ask for one.

10. Always end the call with a polite thank you and goodbye. If the customer is any kind of prospect, keep open the possibility of calling them back another time.

If you follow all of the tips and techniques outlined in this book, you'll be well on your way to being a successful marketeer.